18ᵗʰ
Reg

W9-BOO-902

APR 29 2002

A Kid's Guide to Drawing America™

How to Draw
North
Carolina's
Sights and Symbols

Stephanie True Peters

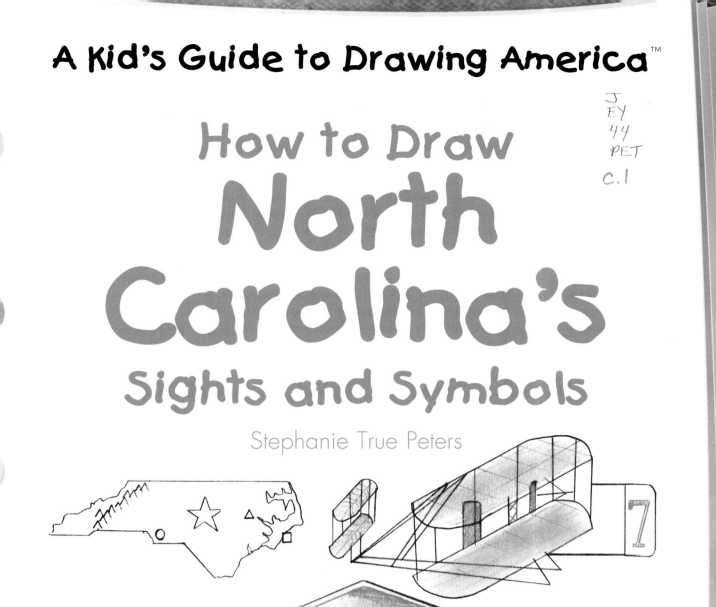

JEY
44
PET
C.1

The Rosen Publishing Group's
PowerKids Press™
New York

Published in 2002 by The Rosen Publishing Group, Inc.
29 East 21st Street, New York, NY 10010

Copyright © 2002 by The Rosen Publishing Group, Inc.

All rights reserved. No part of this book may be reproduced in any form without permission in writing from the publisher, except by a reviewer.

First Edition

Editor: Jannell Khu
Book Design: Kim Sonsky
Layout Design: Nick Sciacca

Illustration Credits: Jamie Grecco
Photo Credits: p. 7 © National Gallery Collection; By kind permission of the Trustees of the National Gallery, London/CORBIS; pp. 8–9 © Morris Museum of Art, Augusta, Georgia; pp. 12, 14 © One Mile Up, Incorporated; pp. 16, 20 © Gary W. Carter/CORBIS; p. 18 © David Muench/CORBIS; p. 22 © Bettmann/CORBIS; p. 24 © Mark Gibson/CORBIS; p. 26 © Michael Maconachie; Papilio/CORBIS; p. 28 © Index Stock.

Peters, Stephanie True, 1965–
How to draw North Carolina's sights and symbols / Stephanie True Peters.
p. cm. — (A kid's guide to drawing America)
Includes index.
Summary: This book explains how to draw some of North Carolina's sights and symbols, including the state seal, the official flower and the Cape Hatteras Lighthouse.
  ISBN 0-8239-6089-7
1. Emblems, State—North Carolina—Juvenile literature 2. North Carolina—In art—Juvenile literature 3. Drawing—Technique—Juvenile literature [1. Emblems, State—North Carolina 2. North Carolina 3. Drawing—Technique]
I. Title   II. Series
  2002
743'.8'99756—dc21

Manufactured in the United States of America

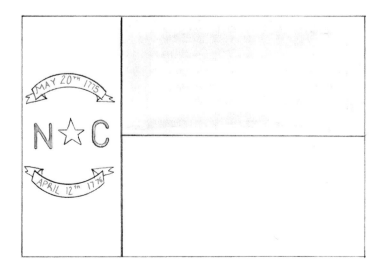

CONTENTS

Let's Draw North Carolina

If you have clothes made in the United States, there's a good chance that they were made in North Carolina. North Carolina leads the nation in clothing production. North Carolina also makes more wooden furniture than does any other state. North Carolina is home to the largest research facility in the nation, the 7,000-acre (2,833-ha) Research Triangle Park.

North Carolina is filled with interesting places. In the northeast corner is the Great Dismal Swamp, a huge region so wild and dangerous that few people have explored it. Located in eastern North Carolina in Croatan Sound, Roanoke Island holds a mystery more than four centuries old. In 1587, a group of colonists who had settled on the island returned to England to get supplies. When they returned three years later, all the colonists in the colony they'd left behind had disappeared from Roanoke Island without a trace! To this day, no one knows what happened to the settlers.

The Great Smoky Mountains National Park sits on

the North Carolina–Tennessee border. This is one of the most-visited parks in the nation. Bears, elk, deer, and other animals call this park home. Its 800 square miles (2,072 sq km) are filled with trees, plants, and animals. In this book, you will learn how to draw some of North Carolina's interesting sights and symbols. Clear directions and illustrations lead you through each drawing step by step. Each new step is shown in red. Carefully study each step before you begin. You will need the following supplies to draw North Carolina's sights and symbols:

- A sketch pad
- An eraser
- A number 2 pencil
- A pencil sharpener

These are some of the shapes and drawing terms you need to know to draw North Carolina's sights and symbols:

 3-D box

 Shading

Almond shape

 Squiggle

Horizontal line

Teardrop

 Oval

Vertical line

 Rectangle

Wavy line

The Tar Heel State

No one knows exactly how North Carolina got its nickname, the Tar Heel State. Tar is a sticky, black substance made from coal or wood. One story has it that during the American Revolution (1775–1783), British troops led by General Cornwallis were about to cross what is now known as the Tar River between Rocky Mount and Battleboro. The North Carolina colonists dumped tar into the river to prevent the British from crossing. When the British went into the river, they got "tar heels," or feet covered with tar! North Carolina has another nickname, the Old North State. From 1629 to 1710, the areas of North Carolina and South Carolina were not divided. This area was known simply as Carolina. The name "Carolina" comes from the name *Carolus*. *Carolus* is Latin for "Charles." Carolina was named for King Charles I of England. When Carolina was divided into North Carolina and South Carolina in 1710, people started calling North Carolina the Old North State, because it was the older settlement of the two.

North Carolina and South Carolina were named after King Charles I of England, shown here on horseback. The name "Charles" is *Carolus* in Latin.

Artist in North Carolina

Elliott Daingerfield (1859–1932) was born in Harpers Ferry, West Virginia, but he is considered one of North Carolina's important artists. He grew up in Fayetteville, North Carolina, and spent his summers from 1886 to 1932 in Blowing Rock, North Carolina.

Elliott Daingerfield

At age 21, Daingerfield moved to New York City to study art. While there he studied under George Inness and Albert Pinkham, two of America's most gifted landscape artists. Daingerfield's art career took place at a time when many of America's suburbs were developing into cities. During this time, Daingerfield captured landscapes that were still unspoiled by development. His most important landscapes were of the Blue Ridge

Daingerfield drew *Sketch of Trees* with graphite on paper. The sketch is undated.

Mountains in North Carolina. One of his favorite subjects to paint was Grandfather Mountain, the highest peak in the Blue Ridge Mountains. Daingerfield painted different views of this mountain for more than 46 years! Grandfather Mountain is the subject and the name of the watercolor below, but the clouds, mist, and artist's use of light are just as important as the mountain itself. Notice that the mist covers most of the mountain. Daingerfield included these elements to show the natural, atmospheric conditions unique to the Blue Ridge Mountains.

Grandfather Mountain, N.C. was painted between 1910 and 1920 and measures 9 ¼" x 13 ¼ " (23 cm x 34 cm). It is a watercolor on paper. Toward the end of his life, Daingerfield had three studios near Blowing Rock, North Carolina, including a studio built on a hillside that overlooked Grandfather Mountain.

Map of North Carolina

Map of the Continental United States

North Carolina is bordered by the Atlantic Ocean and the states of Tennessee, Virginia, South Carolina, and Georgia. North Carolina is divided into three regions. The mountain region is in the west. This is where you can find the Appalachian Mountains, which span from Georgia to Maine. The Great Smoky Mountains and the Blue Ridge Mountains of western North Carolina are two links in this long mountain chain. The Piedmont region is in the state's center. This area has rural farmland, busy towns, and cities. The Atlantic Coastal Plain region is in the east. This region has beaches, marshland, and miles of pine forest and flat plains. The state's climate is mild, but can be very cold in the mountains and warm on the coast.

1

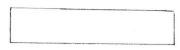

Start with a rectangle. This shape is a guide to help you draw North Carolina.

2

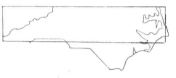

Study the red lines before you draw. Pay careful attention to the eastern part of the state. The southern part of the state needs to jut downward.

3

Erase extra lines. Draw a circle for Charlotte and a triangle for Croatan National Forest.

4

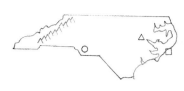

For Cape Hatteras, draw a square. Draw several shapes that look like this /\ for the Great Smoky Mountains.

5

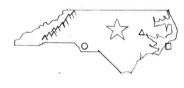

Draw a star to mark Raleigh, the capital city of North Carolina.

6

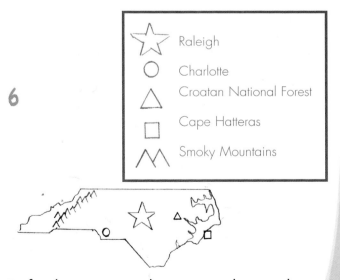

To finish your map, draw a map key on the upper right corner. These are the key places you just drew.

The State Seal

North Carolina's first seal was adopted in 1893. It went through several changes until the current seal was adopted in 1971. On the left, the figure of Liberty holds a scroll and a pole with a liberty cap on top. The figure of Plenty, on the right, holds a sheaf of grain in one hand. She rests her other hand on a horn filled with fruits and vegetables, which stand for North Carolina's rich agriculture. In the background are mountains and the ocean.

The date, May 20, 1775, is when Mecklenburg County, North Carolina, declared independence from Great Britain. The state motto, *esse quam videri*, is Latin for "to be, rather than to seem." It is written in the outer circle of the seal. The words "The Great Seal of the State of North Carolina" are written on the seal's outer circle.

1

Draw two large circles. Inside these circles, draw two small ovals. Notice the placement of the ovals.

2

Study the shapes highlighted in red before you draw them. Start with the left figure.

3

Start with the left figure. Draw her arms and her neck. Then add the details of her clothing. Then work on the right figure. Draw her arms, her neck, and her feet. Erase extra lines.

4

Shape the heads of the two women. Add a circle and a triangle for the horn.

5

Add hair and faces. Draw Liberty's staff, cap, and scroll. Draw Plenty's wheat sheaf.

6

Write the words that are in the border of the seal. Write the date in the seal's center. Draw mountains, the ocean, the ship, and the horn's contents. Shade the areas shown in red.

The State Flag

On the left of North Carolina's flag is a vertical blue bar and to the right are horizontal red and white bars. The letters N and C stand for North Carolina. The date, May 20, 1775, is when Mecklenburg County, North Carolina, declared independence from Great Britain. April 12, 1776, is when the whole colony of North Carolina voted for independence.

North Carolina's flag hasn't changed since it was adopted in 1885. In 1907, North Carolina's government passed a law to have the state flag flown from all state buildings, including schools and courthouses. That way people would see it whenever they passed one of those buildings!

1

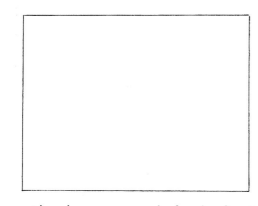

Start with a large rectangle for the flag's field.

2

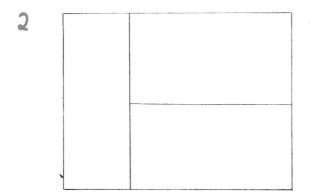

Divide the flag into three parts with a vertical line and a horizontal line. Notice the placement of these two lines.

3

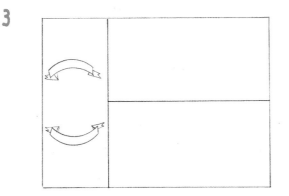

Draw two curved rectangles for the banners. Now draw the ends of the banners.

4

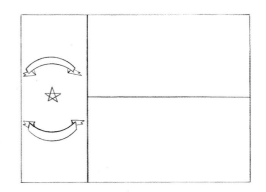

Add a star between the banners.

5

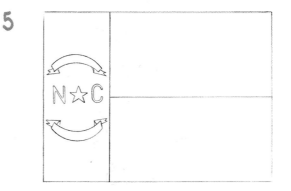

Erase extra lines. Write the letters *N* and *C* on either side of the star. These letters stand for North Carolina.

6

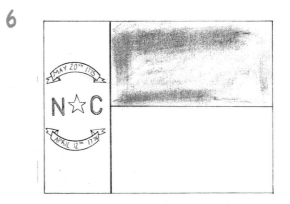

Shade or color your flag, and you're done. Write "May 20th 1775" on the upper banner and "April 12th 1776" on the lower banner.

The Dogwood Flower

The dogwood flower became North Carolina's state flower in 1941. It grows on a tree called the flowering dogwood (*Cornus florida*). When you see the  white or pale pink blossoms on a dogwood, you will think that they are the flower petals. They are not petals but leaves, called bracts. Bracts protect the real flowers that grow at the bracts' center. The flowers are tiny. They are greenish yellow and grow in clusters. Even though the bracts are not flowers, they make the dogwood tree look beautiful in the spring. The dogwood tree produces berries in the late summer. When birds pass through North Carolina as they migrate south for the winter, they eat the berries to get an energy boost.

1

Start with a small circle.

2

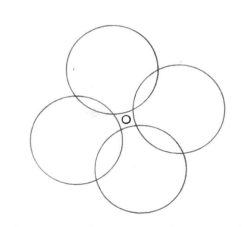

Draw larger overlapping circles around the center circle. These are the bracts.

3

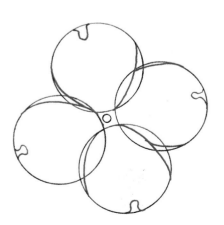

Use the circles as guides to draw the shape of the bracts.

4

Erase extra lines so your drawing looks like the above.

5

For the tiny cluster of flowers, draw a thin rectangle shape and add a small oval shape on top of it. Continue to draw this shape until you have a cluster.

6

Add shading and detail to your flower, and you're done!

The Pine

The pine tree became North Carolina's state tree in 1963. The pine is a type of tree known as a conifer. Conifers have needles instead of leaves. Pine trees are evergreens, which means they don't lose their needles, and they stay green year-round. Today forests cover 60 percent of North Carolina's total area and consist mainly of pines.

When settlers first came to colonize North Carolina in 1663, they cut down pine trees to build houses. Later turpentine, tar, and lumber were made from pines and were sold to merchants. These products were also sold to the navy to use to keep their ships in top shape. Pine wood is still used to build houses and other wood products, such as furniture.

1

Start with a long, thin triangle for the tree trunk.

2

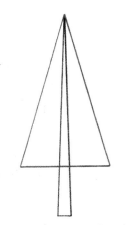

Draw a wide triangle over the thin triangle.

3

Draw curvy lines from the tree trunk to the edge of the wide triangle. These are the tree's branches.

4

Fill in the triangle with branches. When you're done, erase the triangle.

5

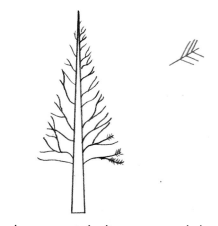

Draw short, straight lines on each branch for the tree's needles. Look at the close-up of the needles. To make the tree look full, draw needles on all the branches.

6

Shade the tree and add some grass. You're done!

The Cardinal

The cardinal became North Carolina's state bird on March 4, 1943. Cardinals have a tuft of longer feathers on top of their heads called a crest. It's easy to spot the male cardinal because he is bright red. The female is brownish in color with only splashes of red on her crest, wings, and tail. Both the male and the female have red beaks and black coloring around their eyes and underneath their bills.

The cardinal is sometimes known as the winter redbird, because its red feathers stand out so clearly against the white snow. The cardinal is a songbird. Unlike many kinds of songbirds, both the male and the female cardinals sing. You can find cardinals in North Carolina year-round.

1

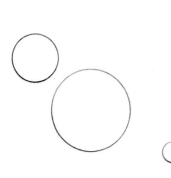

Draw three circles. Notice the size and the placement of the circles.

2

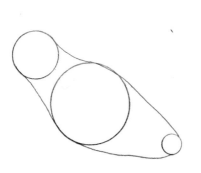

Draw curved lines to connect the three circles. Erase extra lines.

3

For the wing, draw two angled lines that meet at a point. For the tail, draw a thin triangle. Erase extra lines.

4

Draw two triangles, one for the bird's beak and another for the bird's crest. Erase extra lines.

5

Draw the bird's legs and feet. Add an almond shape for the bird's eye. Draw a shape that looks like this > in the beak area.

6

Draw a line through the beak. Add shading and detail to your cardinal, and you're done.

21

The Wright Brothers

On December 17, 1903, Orville Wright made history when he flew the world's first motorized airplane at Kitty Hawk, North Carolina. The Wright brothers, Orville and Wilbur, designed and built the wood and fabric plane. Kitty Hawk, with its strong winds and sandy beaches, seemed like the ideal place to fly their creation. The Wright brothers hoped the wind would help keep their plane in the air. They hoped the sand would soften the blow if the plane crashed! The flight lasted for 12 seconds, reached 10 feet (3 m) off the ground, and traveled only 120 feet (36.5 m). Yet the flight was a success, because it was the start of modern air transportation. The Wright Memorial at Kitty Hawk marks this historic feat.

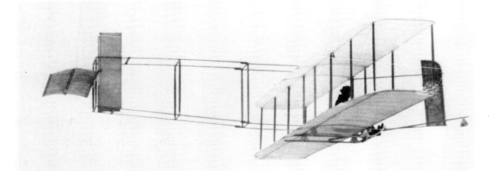

1

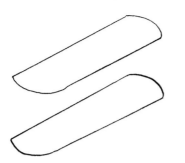

First draw the two shapes as shown above for the airplane's wings. Notice that they look like rectangles with rounded ends.

2

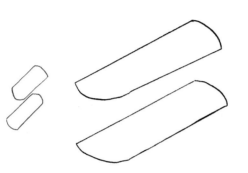

Add two smaller rectangles with rounded ends for the tail. Note the placement of the small rectangles.

3

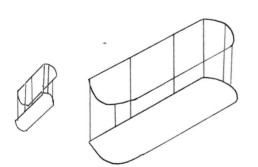

Connect the rectangles with thirteen vertical lines.

4

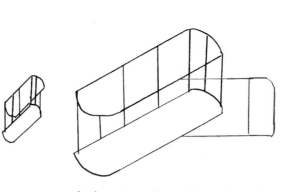

Draw a rounded rectangle to the right of the wings. Connect the rectangle to the wings with two horizontal lines.

5

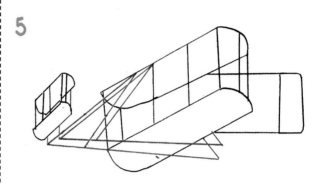

Use straight lines to draw the bars that connect the wings to the tail. Study the lines before you start.

6

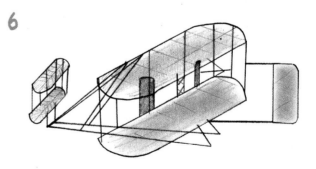

Add three rectangle shapes between the wings. Shade the airplane and you are done!

Cape Hatteras Lighthouse

The Cape Hatteras Lighthouse was built in 1803. The lighthouse helped ships make their way through the dangerous waters near the Outer Banks, along the eastern coast of North Carolina. A second lighthouse was built in 1870, because the first one was damaged during the Civil War (1861–1865). Black and white stripes were painted on the lighthouse in 1873, so sailors could see it better in the daytime.

Over time waves washed away the earth near the shore, making it dangerous to have a tall building there. At 208 feet (63 m) tall, Cape Hatteras Lighthouse is the tallest lighthouse in the United States. In 1998, the lighthouse was closed down and was moved 2,900 feet (884 m) farther away from the ocean. It reopened on May 26, 2000.

1

Draw a large, thin triangle with a flat top. This is the basic shape of the lighthouse.

2

Draw two short, slanted vertical lines on top of the basic shape of the lighthouse. Now add a small, thin rectangle on top of the lines. Notice the shape looks like a flower pot.

3

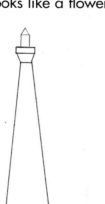

Draw a small rectangle at the top of the lighthouse. Then add a triangle to the top of this rectangle.

4

Draw two thin, horizontal rectangles at the bottom of the lighthouse. Now draw two thin, vertical rectangles.

5

Erase extra lines. Add a small circle to the top of the roof. Use diagonal lines to draw stripes across the lighthouse.

6

Add shading and detail to your lighthouse, and you're done!

The Gray Squirrel

The gray squirrel became North Carolina's official state mammal in 1969. This gray rodent can be seen throughout North Carolina wherever trees are found. That includes the mountain region and the Atlantic Coastal Plain region with its marshy coastlands and forests. You can also find squirrels in city parks and backyards. Gray squirrels live in the trees and build nests of leaves. Gray squirrels don't hibernate, but they do bury acorns and nuts in holes in the ground to eat during the cold winter months. Though they are most at home in trees, gray squirrels can swim in calm water. They can swim up to 2 miles (3 km), if they have to!

1

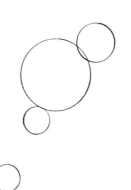

Start by drawing four circles for the body and the tip of the tail. Notice the size and the placement of the circles.

2

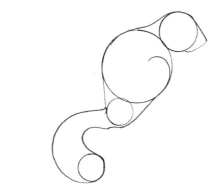

Use curved lines to connect the circles to form the shape of the squirrel's body and tail.

3

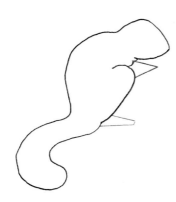

Erase extra lines. Add two small triangles for the squirrel's front and back legs.

4

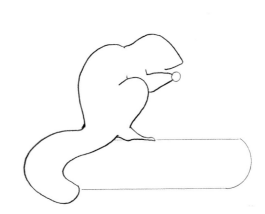

Shape the triangles you just drew so your squirrel looks like the drawing above. Draw a circle of its paw and add detail to its foot. Draw the three lines for the log.

5

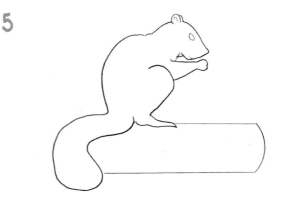

Draw three curved shapes for the ears. Draw an almond shape for the eye and a small curved line for the mouth.

6

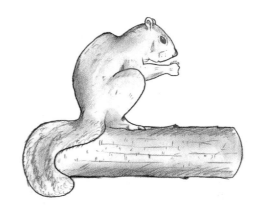

Add shading and detail to the squirrel and the log. You're done!

North Carolina's Capitol

In 1792, Raleigh was established as North Carolina's capital city. The state's capitol building was completed in 1840. The building is one of the finest and the best-preserved examples of Greek Revival architecture in the United States.

North Carolina's government made a very difficult decision inside this building. In April 1861, the Civil War started in South Carolina. Soon after that, President Abraham Lincoln ordered troops from North Carolina to fight against troops from South Carolina. North Carolina refused. The state's legislature voted to separate from the Union and join the Confederate States of America rather than fight against their Southern neighbors.

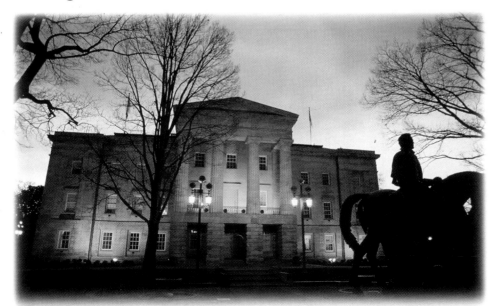

1

Start with three rectangles for the building's wings. Notice that the middle rectangle is wider than the other two.

2

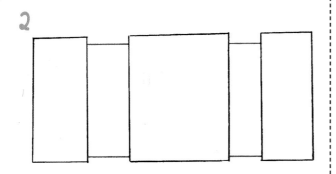

Use horizontal lines to connect the rectangles.

3

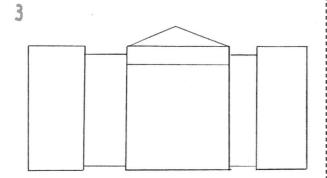

Use two straight lines to form a triangle on top of the middle rectangle. Draw a straight line across the bottom part of the largest rectangle.

4

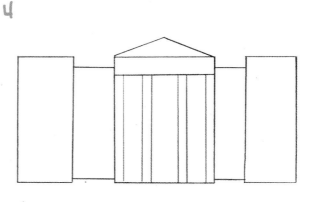

Draw six vertical lines for the building's columns.

5

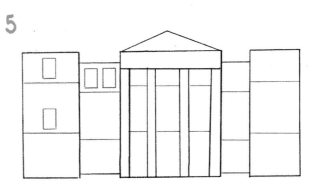

Draw two horizontal lines across each wing. Add several rectangle shapes. These will be the windows and the doors of the building.

6

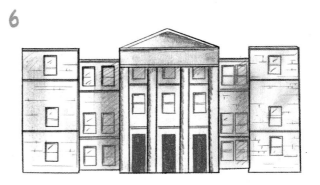

Finish the windows and doors, and add shading and detail to your building. Notice that some parts of the building are darker than others.
Good job!

29

North Carolina State Facts

Statehood	November 21, 1789, 12th state
Area	52,672 square miles (136,420 sq km)
Population	8,049,300
Capital	Raleigh, population, 243,800
Most Populated City	Charlotte, population, 416,300
Industries	Textiles, tobacco products, chemicals, furniture, computers
Agriculture	Apples, blueberries, tobacco, beef cattle, turkeys, chickens, corn
Nicknames	The Tar Heel State; the Old North State
Motto	*Esse quam videri*, To Be, Rather Than To Seem
Precious Stone	Emerald
Rock	Granite
Insect	Honeybee
Animal	Gray squirrel
Bird	Cardinal
Reptile	Eastern box turtle
Fish	Channel bass
Shell	Scotch bonnet
Flower	Dogwood flower
Tree	Pine

Glossary

adopted (uh-DOPT-ed) To have accepted or approved something.

American Revolution (uh-MER-uh-ken reh-vuh-LOO-shun) Battles that soldiers from the colonies fought against England for freedom.

atmospheric (at-muh-SFEER-ik) Having to do with the character or the mood of a place.

Civil War (SIH-vul WOR) The war fought between the northern and southern states of America from 1861 to 1865.

Confederate States (kuhn-FEH-duh-ret STAYTS) States that fought for the South during the Civil War.

conifer (KA-nih-fur) An evergreen tree that bears cones, such as pine, spruce, or fir.

Greek Revival style (GREEK rih-VY-vuhl STYL) An architectural style imitating elements of ancient Greek temple design, popular in the United States and Europe in the first half of the nineteenth century.

hibernate (HY-bur-nayt) To stay inside during a cold period of time.

legislature (LEH-jus-lay-chur) A group of elected people that have the power to make the laws of a state or country.

liberty cap (LIH-ber-tee KAP) A hat that stands for freedom of speech.

motorized (MOH-ter-yzd) Something that moves with the use of a motor or an engine, such as a car or an airplane.

Outer Banks (OW-tur BANKS) A long chain of islands that runs along the entire coast of North Carolina.

rodent (ROH-dent) A small animal, usually with sharp teeth for chewing.

sheaf (SHEEF) A group of grasses or other plants that are bound together.

turpentine (TER-pen-tyn) An oil made from pine trees that is used to thin paint.

Union (YOON-yun) The northern states that stayed loyal to the federal government during the Civil War.

unique (yoo-NEEK) Being one of a kind.

Index

Web Sites

To find out more about North Carolina, check out these Web sites:
www.50states.com/ncarolin.htm
http://statelibrary.dcr.state.nc.us